salmonpoetry

Diverse Voices from Ireland and the World

ABOUT THE AUTHOR'S PREVIOUS BOOK, *The Sistine Gaze* (2015)

Seamus Cashman lets us partake of the very moment when his single long poem began. Re-visiting the Sistine Chapel, ... his eyes fall on a painted figure ... "...As I stare she seems to invite me to converse". The resulting 'conversation' is [this] extraordinarily ambitious poem ... [The] period and technical details work well, but Cashman's Michelangelo sometimes also shades interestingly into a more future-aware voice, melding – I think – with the poet's own voice. ... ... Cashman's verse has a Whitmanesque quality (the long lines) and can bring to mind Blake's Prophetic Books. Many verses ... celebrate the sexuality of "Eve 'n Adam'... And alongside this, the poem works towards a modern – or perhaps it's a Blakean – godless vision of human life .... Cashman ekphrastically takes on the Sistine Chapel and then writes God out of the picture. ... ... Likewise, The Sistine Gaze concludes its frequent lauding of human sexuality with a recognition of the plain fact of its opposite, death ... Cashman here allows the white space ... work its magic ... creating a rhythm and a chain-link of tensions which add to the reader's experience.

—MARTYN CRUCEFIX, *Agenda Poetry Journal*, UK, 2019

'... a complex and ambitious book, a major achievement, really. "Such beauty and its solitude are radical" and "Until we discover the next word" are two sections that have really entrapped me with their fine construction, thought, and even finer sensibility... A master work. and major achievement, ... of importance in its philosophical, cultural and artistic markings of the Irish historical flow out of which it was written, and as a unique meditation and landmark poem, arising out of a time of significant turnings in Irish society. A poem that belongs to its Irish and European cultural genesis as well as to the Sistine masterpiece by Michelangelo.'

—Poet THOMAS MCCARTHY, launching the book in Dublin 2015

I was totally taken over ... the cumulative effect and total import is magnificent. This is an inspired work, and obviously had that angel sitting at the poet's shoulder!

—ELIZABETH HEALY, former editor *Ireland of the Welcomes*

Quite one of the most astonishing books of the year was Seamus Cashman's long poem about creation and creativity, The Sistine Gaze... ... A long poem is not a merely lyric line written long. It is a thing unto itself, demanding new responses ... Cashman carries this task to a wonderful conclusion. ... Perhaps the most important poetry publication of 2015, The Sistine Gaze will be, is, a landmark in Irish literature.

—PETER COSTELLO, Books Editor, *Irish Catholic Review* 2015

This ekphrastic epic is orchestral, impressionistic, thought-provoking, inviting us, 'To balance life with death and venture bravely to be beautiful.' Human certainty, death and the artist at work are central strands. Cashman has written a masterpiece on Michelangelo's masterpiece. This compelling contemplative poem will fix you in its gaze and transform your very concept of art, poetry, and human genius."

—Mary Swander, Poet Laureate of Iowa, USA

Drawing together threads of the religious, philosophical, artistic, and technical, [Cashman] weaves an approachable and altogether human tapestry against which we may appreciate the triumph the chapel frescoes represent.

—*World Literature Today*, University of Oklahoma

The frescoes on the Sistine Chapel ceiling are starting points for Cashman's thoughts, which often incorporate present day technology ... as well as Irish legends: ... myths and figures include Leda, Jonah and the Whale, the Flood, Venus, Aphrodite, Plato, Cuchulainn, Cleopatra, 'Medbh Morrigan Magdalene'...[He] has an ear for sound, and takes pleasure in word-lists: "squirm, brim, broth, brew; / loosen, stretch, streamline, strew" ... this collection isn't about constraint ... Think Ginsberg... There is something endearing about his self-deprecation, self-mocking bombast ... especially when, in 'The grip of the uncanny,' he writes ... in beautifully rhythmic lines. ... Cashman emerges as a personality with a highly developed sensual bawdiness, self-doubt and generous human sympathies ... sheer verve and exuberance...

—Afric McGlinchey, *Southword Journal*

The Sistine Gaze engages imaginatively and intellectually with Michelangelo's frescoes and this demands scale and execution of a high order; it requires a more than usual organisation of sources, religious, philosophical, biblical, mythological, and artistic. The fruitful interaction of the parts, the changing music of the lines, and the dynamic linking of images carry the work forward in lyrical, descriptive and dramatic modes. The poem illuminates an entire process of seeing and understanding.

—Dr. Maurice Harmon, Emeritus Professor, UCD

[Cashman's} latest book of poetry is a masterwork -... an almost stream of consciousness .... I googled the various images from the Sistine, and while this was visually informative, I couldn't progress ... So I returned to the poetry and read and read and left the words build their images, and I stopped seeking sense and structure. At times, this was amazing and exciting. At other times, I was lost in history [&] myth ... Book 1 Creation is a blast of energy, and it was sexy. A section (We are Awake) wowed me with Joycean fun and the power of words. Cashman has the words and he plasters high heaven with his ambition.

—Liam Murphy, *Munster Express*

BY THE SAME AUTHOR

POETRY

The Sistine Gaze: I too begin with scaffolding (Salmon Poetry, 2015);
also, limited illustrated edition (The Otherworld Press, 2015)

That morning will come: new & selected poems (Salmon Poetry, 2007)

Clowns & Acrobats (Wolfhound Press, 2000)

Carnival (Monarchline, 1987)

Probe: poems by CB Quarterman: with Tom Conaty, Daragh Bradish & Paul Bregazzi
(The Otherworld Press, 2014)

ANTHOLOGIES

Poems for Mamilla: editor. The English language poems from the Mamilla International Poetry Festival, Ramallah,
2013; with the Mahmoud Darwish Museum & ARCH (The Otherworld Press & ARCH, 2014)

Something beginning with P: new poems by Irish poets, editor (The O'Brien Press, 2004; 2008)
Selected edition: *P is for Poetry* (The O'Brien Press, 2020)

The Wolfhound Book of Irish Poems for Young People, editor with Bridie Quinn. Illus. (Wolfhound Press, 1975).
Paperback as, *Irish Poems for Young People (*Wolfhound, 1982, 1987, 1990, 2000, 2003)

OTHER WORKS

On the Nature of Disagreement: Reformations Within, after Martin Luther's '95 Theses,
co-ed with Tom Conaty (The Otherworld Press, 2017)

Folktales from Likonde: Tanzania 1967-Ireland 2017, with poems by Seamus Cashman
The Otherworld Press, 2017)

Cré na hÉireann Creating Common Ground: The Story of the Mound. With Tom Conaty
(Otherworld Press, 2014, 2017. New ed. 2020)

Step Together– From Pillar to Spire: Citizens Day (The Otherworld Press, 2005, 2006)

Proverbs & Sayings of Ireland, with Sean Gaffney. Illus. by Billy Merwick (Wolfhound Press, 1975-2003) Also,
2003 edition with illustrations by Robert Gibbings. As, *Irish Proverbs & Sayings: new gift eds* (The O'Brien
Press: 2015; & illustrated ed. 2019)

the arts council
an chomhairle ealaíon

funding literature
artscouncil.ie

Talking down the clock
& other poems

by

Seamus Cashman

salmonpoetry

Published in 2023 by

Salmon Poetry

Cliffs of Moher, County Clare, Ireland

Website: www.salmonpoetry.com

Email: info@salmonpoetry.com

Copyright © Seamus Cashman, 2023

ISBN 978-1-912561-71-1

All rights reserved. No part of this publication may be reproduced or transmitted in any form or by any means, electronic or mechanical, including photography, recording, or any information storage or retrieval system, without permission in writing from the publisher. The book is sold subject to the condition that it shall not, by way of trade or otherwise, be lent, resold or otherwise circulated without the publisher's prior consent in any form of binding or cover other than that in which it is published and without a similar condition, including this condition, being imposed on the subsequent purchaser.

Cover: See notes on page 126

Cover Design & Typesetting: Siobhán Hutson

Printed in Ireland by Sprint Print

Salmon Poetry gratefully acknowledges the support of
The Arts Council / An Chomhairle Ealaíon

Contents

I
Notebook Exits

I

We all end in metaphor

'the achievement of intimacy' (Ted Cohen)

Fairy tales laying ghosts reassure
that all is well and will end so.
But temporality conceals the lie
of land's unrealised anticipations.

Crossing a sunset border
beyond and behind the chronic
ticking of this unremitting clock,
we lean on unknown boundaries,
precursors to gravity's collapse.

Like music, poetry or pictures
on a wall we strive to understand,
there is a quantum leap to soul.

Do me so do – so me do – me...
Ecstasy without a beating heart
this rainfall music of the spheres.
Down,
       down,
              down – to silence.

Coffined, abandoned or burnt,
we all end in metaphor.

II

Sórt aisling óg

Ón tús
cosaí dána a bhí ann.
ag sár-siúil siar mo bhóthar.
Cosaí tapaig dhána.
agus gúna leo
gúna fíor-dhána
gan dabht –
Mo chroí, mo chroí.
bhfuil fághta dhom
ach uaighneas an leaba
uaighneas ón mbórd;
uaighneas im intinn dom.
Cosaí dána, a chailín.
Mór mo ghraidhin thú!

(English translation in end-notes.)

III

Likonde ebony

In the kitchen on a side table overlooked
by once pretentious ceramic table lamps
– one brown, cracked and taped for use,
the other lilac with sculpted porthole –
sit old magazines, a plastic pencil case,
biros, tape dispenser, sunglasses,
a yellow post-it pad, my grey hoodie helmet
and a steel ruler on a dark green cutting board.

Here too forever waits,
far from her Likonde home, in ebony bust
with jutting chinbone, flattened nose,
solid set-back ears, and, tight-cropped,
a densely swirling shoal of hair.
Hooded eyes flesh blinds of darkness;
and from her high muscular neck, solemn
angular lips mediate with pride
a noble tilted head.

And though at a distance and off-grid,
there is no distance for in spells
of doubt, she is sustenance.

IV

I spent my life making books
– other people's books. Fuck other people
and other people's books. But the making
of those books was good. I stopped
making other people's books
stopped the making that was good
to make my own muck my own sort of fuck.

And found it good to wallow in,
better than other people's suck.
When the sun shone I spread it out
to dry. My muck.
Muck dries up nicely in the sun
its polygonic discs crackle underfoot
in desiccated empty desert rhymes
of wilted words and fractures.

All those dead metaphors
and flailing rhythmic spines
of never-ending gob-stopped lines.

Go, trot across the squelchless souk
to dunk your own rhymes.

V

Curator:

Midway, here on this wall,
lurks an ordinary office stationary press.

Inside, long abandoned documents reside
with laptops, desktops, cables, floppy discs
– and odds and ends.

No tabernacle this loner here;
no longer noticed; never pried.
A chimera

This wall too
seems ...

                    uncertain

VI

in a high wind
limbs brace and stiffen
and you might arch
your back fearful of catastrophe

fingers will squelch
the thick mud, and toes
bleed on sharp rubble
gasping for breath

in rising tides
hold the flush of energy
be slow to let go
of fading light

VII

On reading Niall Quinn's Welcome to Gomorrah

He remembered telling her, the timid mouse,
that he wanted to be an elephant
in Africa.
But here in Brazil
Ilana was already soundly sleeping.

Her nightmare came again
...no change...her legs
kicked and kicked
awash with sweat
and only broken words, broken sounds
of German – with here and there
a direct sentence of plain schoolbook English.

But she awoke remembering joy:
'Bom dia, mia amo. Bom dia, mia amo.'

In nightmare if I sleep
a passenger train pulls away empty
and its red-bright spangles distract ...

VIII

The supermarket maw

I take the nearest escalator to the next floor.
I don't know why for I have no business here
no ceiling to paint, nor jewellery to buy.
Back-tracking from the post-office,
a whisper in my brain says
'milk, bread and parsnips'
as I pass a supermarket maw.

The threshold crossing splashes me in colour
streams that course through my gullet
to pool as sillion – clumps of clay
in an empty stomach. I stop to get out
my glasses, polish lenses for clarity.

I take stock, already surrounded
by brash countertops of raw meat,
iced fish, rackfulls of root veg and crinkly
lettuce heads. The boldly branded stands
of stuffed bread wrappers screech where they hawk
under a surgical flight of white bulbs.
To my right are the streets of New York
crowded with trolley people. My feet lock.

10.30 of a Wednesday morning
and this flooded byway drenched
under an adhesive glare.
Pocketing my glasses I re-tune,
swivel, hurry out to an escalator
– that slows me –
towards the nearest exit.

IX

Marcel Marceau knew better:
he rendered invisibility.
His angular poised posing
a no-face to seize eyes,
to hold breath;
legs and hands forgotten.
A painter of non-smile shapes;
forget your polka-dots,
he knew the dark,
the visibility of silence
where movement is in shadow
where we are not.

As laughter is strangled,
excitation chokes; the throat
retching wordlessly sucks back in,
engulfed in an expansion of now,
aware of intransigence,
of some inaction ...

X

your manicures are not inconsequential
your multi-colours do not drown
they sparkle strands
of waveblown flicker
crisp and light

my hands breathe differently
touch your shimmer
softly mirror
this concave slender
of your waist

eyes question

XI

Through an observation window
white studio walls, grained wood floor
and shadow figures wait
as if for time. 'Here it is,'
one says. 'Come in – everything's
gonna be alright.'

An unframed wall print
deepens as we pass,
its flag-like red blaze
pixilating into tresses
all on white. Clean. Alive.
We stand inside the door
waiting. The room abuzz
to our performance call,
all eighteen dancers, we now
among them on the floor
as well as watching
from the wall.

Dance colours the flowing silks,
gleaming satins, veils, throws,
skirts and waving sleeves.
Stocking'd feet skip ablaze
all-a-whisper on the floor;
forward, back, turn
and step between.
Graceful. Clean.

Troupes regroup in tentacles
round about, a double line.
Upfront one dancing pair,
tall, upright, and stepping
towards us. Bearded face.
Her arm in his. Her eyes
a multi-coloured net.

All find a still point.

There, dance resumes.
Side by side, step on step
troupes re-spark the flame
and feet enjoy a riff – a riff
so fast those dancers sway within
its mirror-rhythms, lilt con brio
from the floor as bodies soar
treble-high, and free.

XII

To read over dinner,
I brought two love poems
by Michelangelo, and a dark 'Madonna'
with carved lips and slanted cheek curving
her grained ebony profile.
My Tanzania of fifty years.

But some spoor erupted in your irises
spinning heavy whorls
                          that drown
underneath its pyroclastic flow
                          the words
folded in my pocket

XIII

Measurements

– a poem for 28 September

Phase I

The material intractability of measurement,
consequence and interpretation attracts;
but what matters in our immeasurable meridian,
amid players of games and curious crowds,
is birth,
where science and poetry channel.
The rest – like bad rhymes and rotting metres –
practical, political and innocent is, ultimately, meaningless

I count.
– people in rooms, at poetry readings, on the street; steps, objects on
window sill or shelf, cormorants on rocky foreshores, books on my desk,
people at prayer, seats in cinemas, heads.
Not quite obsessively nor all of the time. But often enough.
More consolatory I think – the consolation of practical knowledge
or in some measure, of my mind's understanding of eye.

Phase II

random measurement
may create random movement
or hang us from the rafters

speak
to be spoken to
be silent to hear truth
slide down the balustrade
from atop a cone of words
until you cannot hear the throat
only the whisper of lips and the lapping

of your tongue's hidden movement

September 28 contains a random partial link
with my brain's synaptic conglomerates:
the definition, in 1889, of the metre
as a meridian based distance
at the melting point of ice, between two lines marked
on a standard bar of platinum with ten percent iridium.

That was in the one hundredth year before the birth
of my daughter Aideen in 1989.
– Aideen, the youngest, six characters; Cormac, six; Fergus, six; but Soracha,
the eldest, chose her seven, though christened Sarah, five.
Containing and releasing are creative ways.
Seamus is six. Their mother eight.

Phase III
random numbers find me
            randomly
– this writing is August 28* – for me, O'Flaherty's date
my own October 31 has been denied by the State
my passport tells it 30 (days hath September
April June November) but my mother told me 31
and she mattered all of my diary days.
We measure everything
and hate not being able to fly
we kill brothers and sisters for trifles
I flew the nest before today
tomorrow beat your wings
in serendipity
sing the truth
of destruction that may follow
– it may not.
Your song sung IS song.
Silence will not compose
until you sing

XIV

in early summer
birds flock to ground
for crumbs of a loaf scattered daily.
They perch if forgotten and wait –
nouns adrift in the wind
make time's unveiling visible
conjugating our presence.
It doesn't matter they seem to say,
we don't matter even to ourselves.
Would we become if we could simply be?
The coming is what counts, yet
things that matter are such tiny things
food, breath, movement, sex, and skin
– *that was sin; truly the one sun-song*
in seared syllables offering heat
and dust to crickets at night.
  Cicadas comfort the moonlight;
  abundance in chambers of blood;
  eruptions flood the brain;
  joy mined deep,
and fear.

...oh, shit!
fling out your arms
unbuckle the universe – no better man,
spread those legs   braise those thoughts,
bring i to eye and be upfronted

see me crumple like a suit of clothes
emptied on gravity's encrusting hold
 ... ... am i going or becoming

smaller, smaller,
sliding
into tiny-ness
a spit of difference
here on clay

immaculate in smallness
I am

tiny i am...
   but
  I was
here,
   and
      i took your call

XV

This is my prayer for you –
you who live on margins of belief and beauty
as well as in their depths;
you who walk farms and city streets;
who carry babes in arms and dream destinies:
this is my prayer for you: –

may shadows never fall on your dreams;
may spirits of humankind listen to your voice;
may the touch of generosity caress you;
may moments you cherish be imprinted on your being;
may makers of your dreams taste your sweetnesses.

And if this prayer for you is answered by the universe,
it may in return ask of you:
that you create a new moment for the rest of us;
that in that moment you offer your beloved
generosity in response, thought to absorb,
spirit to host; your body to honour,
laughter to encourage,
pain to inform and to heal,
your wholeness to be in the world's echo.

When this prayer and your understanding of it
find shared space on our planet,
with this song we have to sing together,
and in the music that we make,
each of us might be what we can become.

XVI

He sits toggling screens
She sits plucking age from cheekbones
He sits huddled in a notebook
She stands kneading bread.

    There they are.

When the world walks
stars do not sit still.
As breezes drift through front doors,
the must reveals of leather books disperse.

He had opened the cardboard boxes,
now rubs the whitish mould,
eyeing a goddess blind-blocked
on its mirror wall

She creates the chik-chik chop of knife,
the tangy tep-tep reverb which
wooden spoons claim on the rim
of a saucepan on the ring,
then the on-off tap-rush

the scratching rhythms

of dinner sauce mixed
in a handle-less cup.

In the distance between rooms
doors thud shut.

XVII

Towers weep, people fall;
the air hooshes its howls, stalls,
envelops, traps, hides.

Come. Sing with the planets of collapsed decks.
Wrap our immeasurable expectation
in its skyscraper'd wrecks

Out here skies light up huddled horizon fears;
out there, seas wash clean the bloody spears
that quartered disaster voices: love hate life death.
Hold my hand, night-time; hold my hand; and lead.

With darkness bandaging the womb's wound, bleed
light into the channels and shallows of tomorrow.
Watch remembrance rise to pollinate possibility.
And, then – Song.

September, 2001

XVIII

I love the beauty in faces

the way cheek shadows
lilt as eyes close

how the taut body
probes its chin

how lip muscles leaven
the solemnity of noses

and there – the careless
strand of hair
that sings

XIX

sway me – sway me, sea water swaying
slipping me – slipping me into the deep
depths underneath depths above

here with you – here with you sailing
on waves rolling waves to the beach
to the lapping and spelling the spilling
of limbs on the shore

children all racing their spaces of grace
limbs limbering longingly lambently lift
and cross into splashing, dashing and laughing

contained in the weft of the waves
in the silk of the salt and the rough of the sand
your hand in my hand spelling tales without words
singing songs without sound

we're sliding unpainted down watery pastels
dripping and staining our bodies afloat
in the yellow moon darkness of night
and the sun is away on the far side of water

we flow – we flow on awaiting our tide.
As you open yourself to my now
you breathe me inside you and out

I open myself to your now
I breathe you inside me and out
and we sigh and we see

the silence above is below us
cries from the wind are beneath
what we've told when we kiss
as we sail in the suck of the sway
slipping tales through the deep.

Come with me – come tell me come currents of ether
to bridle our seas with our greens and our reds
we will nourish the sill of the evening slowly and sweet

we rest here immersed in our swaying
we wake – we awake to the scrying of gull
a crane on the shore, a cormorant taut on a rock.

At morning mists lift us and daylight's reveals
set our visions aweigh on the sway of our time
in such stirrings of brine

day or night then or now we're astride
and unfurled in the heat and the light,
the beat in our hearts ever coding and scoring
this living – this loving – language of life.

XX

When washed, our cold stone kitchen floor slabs
hold winter's dampness except by the fireplace.
In summer our feet sometimes surprise
its solidity; the sweeping brush dusts off
breadcrumbs; a dropped milk jug shat-
ter-splatters white caricatures – a face
in profile, an elephant, a bicycle pump,
or just a splash – and sniffs out
the wet stale smell of floor-cloth.
As we sneak downstairs for illicit drinks,
the chill grid of those slabs at night extends
into one gigantic span beneath our foot-soles,
stretching out its walkway for tunes we stall on,
orchestrating knowledge through unseen boundaries
as darkness morphs to the softness of our skin.

XXI

Mountains of clay are difficult to descend or to climb unless
    you unfold time's crevices
and stumble through, losing sight of people latticed in the
    window going to where it is that people go
when music plays on the radio and raindrops threaten from clouds.
Skylines are lines we may untie as we lie heaving on its mountain
    base, uncertain of boggy dank down washes
mapping streams that sparkle underneath, or, where the clouds break,
    over ground.
And down, always down to home that's settled past the turn.
Abreast the flow of days be not for ever lost and silent in valleys
    of the heart.
Jump, Love, jump.
For there and here between pulse, pause and breath, this body hosts
    your every step.

XXII

All I'm thinking of today is getting out of love
and find it setting traps and snares ...
– I wonder where the rabbits are.

Uncle Batty brought me up the hill through Donovan's fields
above the early morning village to check his last night's settings.
Sometimes the rabbit was alive, sometimes dead. Once
he let one go and said as we watched her silent run, 'She'll be ok.'

I bulged with curiosity, sniffed the air like rabbits do, watched the
    hard punch
and the twisting of necks, felt their warm bellies, feared the wild
    eyes and sharp teeth.
– But I didn't need to get out of there.

At home with the catch skinned down to raw thighs and breasts,
the bloody guts for the river, lanky bellies fresh in rows
and all the skins tacked to the back of our garage doors,
I was capital P proud, sorting traps and snares, pegs and binder twine.

Maybe proud now too – but, gone again,
gone without a wave? I stumble on this narrative.
What when tomorrow comes?
All I'm thinking of today is getting out of love.

XXIII

for love is
quadruped
to the fall

1
I rise, lean over,
across & in between
to press on

2
Somewhere in here
is a seahorse spined
sensitive and mysterious
afloat above my thumb
a child lost in contemplation
a gentle flower petalled
in excruciating thorn
absorbed and undisclosed
Around and in-between
The fluted tiles of a kitchen
floor or summerhouse
emerald across the universe
like some ceramic
encyclopaedic skin
shed by a lucky snake
a pettiness just there
on a horizon disappeared

eyeballs burst
into what is not
even looking, and sigh
the egg fossilled in volcanic stone
beak beckoning mudplast
ectoplast – this last echo
millennia beneath skyblue
reflections raw orange blazoned
palms searching texture's mane
in wracklike mirror flame

now I'm ablaze too but cold.
Waiting too but spoiled
by the rays of a living sun
and towelled dry by your
fallow moon, shadowed, gone

3
Razor sharp on the first of April*
this unconstructed i
did not, no no did not salute –

What is yet unknown
remains unknowable in
a curious awareness of no
thing thang thong no
truth thought broth forth
except this – saw it later
hanging on a wall
in some version of Tate
I now forget:
my pedlar, my revenge
and all the world stolen
by thieves hanging from walls
and dropping like spies

O signature eyes!

4
Gingerbread man
woman and bird
flattened against your
imaginary wall
and aerated with stampings
of cake mould cut-outs
configuring in biscuit
reveals and sunlight

a convulsed threat
in silhouette writhing
passionate linkings,
hardening in
avian coils and sex
with a kind of charm
in the eye and fear
in a vulva-less belly

Evening's translucent sky
Lost.   Love
loving in a world's silence
hears whispers
says 'Goodbye'.

* Max Ernst (1891 – died 1 April 1976)

XXIV

This is my daughter here
on the mantelpiece
hosting her graduation scroll.
The gas fire humming yellow
spreads flame-breath airs
in blue of the night voices
and gold-spun rhythms.

– pure jazz in that smile.

Someone said I should frame you.
But you need no gilded stage
to sing. I watch you mediate
Rilke's pacing panther
in the flame's warmth below

XXV

This morning aslant roof tiles
above the kitchen window,
waiting on the starlings nested
under my gabled extension,
a neighbourhood cat out-stared me.
    Snake in a cave / Water and fruit

I grew up in a village house
as child, in suburbia as man.
But when my son moved out
to join his mates, they all
went to live in 'the gaff'.
    Snake in a cave / Water and fruit

Atop a baobab tree, fruit is safe
comforted in its velvety box.
Secure, the cool of evening
well to well source to source
chains knowledge in bespoke limbs.
    Snake in a cave / Water and fruit

The starlings bested the cat
The cat bested me
I still think the house bested the gaff
But the gaff was a baobab tree.

XXVI

His limbered body, pale, limns high
in a moment's still life, a rhyme
before descent.* His feet-first leap
will tear the surface of the pool
and sinking ankles, knees and thighs,
bare buttocks, belly, waist, then chest
immerse his upraised arms. He's gone!
A morning's pearly splash!

What gods conspire to then un-sheath
and urge in this cold water pond
thrills chilled flesh, and powers the heart.
With frenzied fingers, eyes shut tight,
toes flex against the water bed
propel his up-sprung body high,
rupturing the surface skin,
risen boy, resurrected man.

* Rupert Brooke (3 August 1887-23April 1915) at
Byron's Pool with Virginia Woolf and friends.

II
For young worlds

Welcome, Eve

For Ivy, a girl-child newly here

This, Eve, is your morning.

We too arrived here once, and have been waiting
to interleave our routes, to hold your hands.
Perhaps this is why your questing eyes envelop us
and throat and lips voice thoughts you cannot yet phrase:

'Hi there, whoever whatever we are.'

We begin to know you now. We hear you in the night.
We hold you through the day. We twist and turn and dance
our shadows on the nursery walls, assimilate your play;
sometimes, startled momentarily, we pray.

This, Eve, is your day.

And when you sleep and find an inward restfulness
with us, we sit here thinking: Eve.
This world is new again: Things grow.
The sun shines. The earth is ready – lime and loam.

Welcome, Eve. Welcome home.

Magic Whale

A poem for Ruby – to dance and sing along with

Step one two – step one two three
back one two – back one two three
forward and back – off again
catch the wind as you pass by.

So – Ruby, One. And Ruby, Two.
Ruby, Three – Then one more turn.
Begin again.
Ruby, One. And Ruby, Two.
Ruby, Three – Now you are free.

Mornings dance so gracefully
and night is jealous of her light.
Dark embraces quiet night
who then befriends the coming day.

Oh say – Oh say! Where is the dream
that I walked through last night?
In my breast pocket by my heart
where you and love unite.

So – Ruby, One. And Ruby, Two.
Ruby, Three – Then one more turn.
Begin again.
Ruby, One. And Ruby, Two.
Ruby, Three – Now you are free

to sing new songs to dance new steps
to tell new tales to make new poems
full of magic whales.

Step one two – step one two three
back one two – back one two three
forward and back – then off again
Hey! Catch the wind as you pass by.

Embedded in my brain

The whole world sits here, pointing to the stars.
Everywhere else sparkles in the dark and calls on me
to look down at my feet, grounded in a winter sea
in that once upon a time, and once upon a place
where I took a chance. I think it was a fishes' dance

that hurried up the shore waving adventure in my face.
There were songs of praise singing themselves
out there in the bay, and willing me to walk
from old Portmarnock beach to Malahide,
along those rocks that cuddle with the sea.

You'd think it easy, hop and leap, and leap
and hop from rock to rock there and back,
everyday stuff till daylight wakes; routine
all the way. But no, no, no! I slipped and fell.
Let out a yell. Ran back, crabbed out. I nearly died!

But a passing claw with a silver eye pinched my toe and winked.
I got the message, spun around and sang out loud,
'O why go back if there's a front? Why sink
if there's a swim? Hop rocks and carry on.'
Then, that squeaky voice – the winking crab again.

I heard it talk. I really did! A lyric now embedded in my brain:
'Under water, under ground, we creep and crawl. We make our sounds:
We see touch, we hear pain. We taste the truth in every tale.
We're the water, we're the gravel, we're the rocks, seaweed and sand.
We're the ground that welcomes all. So – look around! Look around.'

I looked – down at my feet and scratching there at
a bright white marbly stain, I saw a claw that disappeared.
I never used to listen to rock crabs,
or sand fleas on the beach, or seagull tribes or cormorants
carved upon the shore. But now my eager eyes were lasering

the ground. Curiosity pinched my nose. I hunkered down
to finger all those pimples on the rock. A million there or more.
The rock was cold but silk in parts, gentle to my touch. I wondered too
for other shapes were long, or wide, or prickly, pockmarked or map-like.
It 'welcomes all', that crab had said. Here perhaps is why:

this rocky shore is fossilised – this ground
is hardwired brain, all bumps and knobs and squelchy parts
– like yours or mine. It is an earth song in us all,
an ancient kin, an ancient call to dance and sing
beside a winter sea where you and I are we.

III
Keys from Palestine

Amer's Story

Gaza City January 2009

Is there any reason not to believe me?
Any reason at all.
I say they killed me three times, those machines.
They just came and when my father opened the door,
the bullet killed him. That was the first time I died.
I know many fathers who never died like that.

We were ordered out of the house.
I wanted to stay with my dead father's body.
One said: Get out or we will kill you too.
I understood that so I abandoned my father's body.
It was to be six days before they let me back – in this hot weather?
Machines have taken over their brains.

There was more to come. My little daughter died.
Farah, joy of the whole world,
breast-fed by her mother to give some comfort
as her intestines leak through bullet wounds.
May I ask why? Are there only machines?
That was the second time I died that day.

Sejah, my other daughter, and my brother Abdullah.
They were shot too. That they didn't die
was not the bullets' truth. Fourteen hours and still
wandering in open spaces, we were trying to hide.
Then they released the dogs.
They released dogs ... those machines did.

Someone offered iodine and bandages – but
that was a day later and we still prisoners
They blindfolded and handcuffed me. Took me
for five days. The first three no water, no toilet.

They asked Where's Gilad? How would I know?
All I know are my dead and my living.

Later, we came home.
We came home later.

We looked for eight hours and couldn't find my father.
Then someone saw his foot
sticking out of cacti rubble and dirt.
No room in our house left undamaged.
The broken clock on a bullet-pocked wall silent
Fouad was now dead. Finally dead.

We can bury him now
that the machines are gone.

Who cares about the stolen money, phones, gold, jewellery,
biscuits – anything of value in our home? Who cares.
My delivery van too – a burned-out shell beside the house.
I looked around at the whole wide world, the ground, the sky.
That was the third time I died. That day.
Fouad, my father, Farah joy of the world, and me.

Is there any reason not to believe me?
– Any reason at all.

What there is

For Mamilla Cemetery, Jerusalem

If there is nothing to forget
what do stones remember?

When memory is drowning
who is calling out?

Whose voices murmur – leave us be?

Great are the oceans we ferried on...
And, see: the sands blow from our feet.

As the stars pierce the sky's taut arc,
their lights foment into song.

We sing too.

Silence dilates its pores
to absorb and to leach.

Stone slabs autograph our apogee.
The hard ground embeds.

A fruit stall by the Hebron road

The oranges tumbling down the hillside
acknowledge the place of flowers.
Leaping clumps of dried up grasses that live
in the broken earth, they dust morning's ripeness
from petals not yet awake, sumac, sage...

lupin, poppy, capers white and yellow,
purple toothed orchids, cyclamen, horn
of the gazelle, hyssop, and camomile,
oleander, and a sweet scented rose.

Some settle into little dimpled graves
lie still in a forever stay; and watch
as others bounce and hope on recklessly
downhill to where the valley floor awaits
forever the evicted certainty.

Some stumble through,
expecting the mid-day sun to be theirs.
But it is not. High in its sky, it binds
a heat indifferent to fruitful tissue
or to bruised fibre under broken rinds.

Going to ground

(Bethlehem, 2014)

In that pocketed city
hemmed by wall and watchtower
silhouettes in pale October sky
darken as I exit Al-Azza
for the last bus to Jerusalem's
Gethsemane and Golgotha.

Throat groans, shouts and calling voices
gesticulate from atop the funeral truck,
harangue a hurried crowding street
of men and boys. On the march.
They are paving Ismael's way
with the language of bodies,
– words of anger, beaten words, cries,
the pained calls to the dead, to all the dead.
Their women cry at home.
They are bringing Ismael to ground
where he will lie too many years
too soon. A colonising bullet
plants seed in soft ground,
ground too hard for young or old
to cheer or fear, or wear across their proud backs
as their bodies too pass through the concrete wall.
Impervious. Being their Nakba.

Unsettled, and behind the settler wall
a stranger passing through,
stopped to wait and watch
where the flowing winds turn left
this one night's passing
as Ismael who has tilled and fed forever here
is brought to ground.

Keys: Lifta Voices

When the misted darkness slips away,
sneaking down slopes
to hide from eyes that stare;
when light uplifts in open air
and revels with voices there:
– then, in the bright of day
hearts break once more;
break as they broke in forty eight,
and forty nine, in fifty, fifty one
on and on, in a mosaic of time
and faces, crackling aged wrinkles
round the eyes and door of each home.

As with famine homes on Achill,
abandoned homes on islands
of water or of land, by river, lake
or limestone shale, where shadows hide
when house is home and empty,
people gone

Lifta's homes squat here, and stare.
Still in their aureole of longing,
sunken wells of longing.
Across their stony tellings is
belonging; beneath its stony will,
belonging; upon its empty walls,
belonging.

When all passers-by are home,
Lifta shouts into its sky
stone words, not steel nor gas,
stone kitchen words of home
that Lifta voices know.

Caoineadh Amjed of Beit Omar

(Lament for Amjed of Beit Omar)

A blush of wind poppy each sunset. Olive trees are brother and sister.
In the rain, holding palms full of fears, stand father and mother.
That day was your last. Now you stride through the past
tense in all of our languages. Strong man and boy.
Your route knows the truth beyond lies, and the cowardice of apartheid.
Woven in memory hoops, the ghost of a speckled mare priding beside you.
Summer flowers on your grave. A key in your pocket for Palestine.

IV
Daily Breaks

Day 1

What I would like to have said at cockcrow next day

'O, shut up, Cock! Shut the shit up!
We're sick of the daily aggravation,
of your pathetic morning orisons.
You're no nymph. No muezzin tones in you.
Be off! Down the yard. Check out your hens.'

BUT I was only four – curious and free
at the boreen end of the Curraheen haggard.
And my busy granny couldn't see.
          'I've had it, traitor. The pot for you. The pot.
Let's see if you can resurrect.'

          'Look at yourself, Cock, so
          proud on dirty cow-soiled clumps of straw,
          raucous, betimes all night, stiffly flapping
          wings out wide; you high-stepping stony craw.'
And – in panic flight – I slip and fall, flat on my back.

O I remember you crowing on top of me
claw-standing, raw feathering my panting chest.
I stopped screaming Cock, but not you, not you.

          'Shut up, Cock. Shut up!
          Cock a-doodle-do... to you!'

Journeying

there's a motorway in-between
and always a far side for those
who sit naked in the kitchen
out of traffic, eating apples.

There are ramps and slipways
no end to this end-without-world world
of waysides we know; we carry on.
Toss the core out of some window.

We eat cooking apples in galleys
drifting toward their own horizons
as we bounce off unforgiving gutters
that lie sinister to our perigee.

Maybe take the next exit south
where word-falls hide out to blood
the chilly isolated routes we fake
on this side of burnt-out rubber.

Day 3

'Blue surrounds me'

(First line of a postcard poem in my letterbox, from "Rebecca".)

Blue surrounds me
the blue of topaz by your ears
of sky beneath the clouds
of shirts I wear
of night
the blue of blues closing
down my sleep
yet when I wake
the sky is greyish white
as all the blue seeps
through my chest and belly
out my fingertips and toes
until the mirror by the stairs
mocks my eejit pose,
constrains the blue
sizes and seizes my down
before signing me out.

Goodbye

Is there a simple way to be?
A way where eyes delight
unquestioningly as ears
absorb and toss about
the rhythms of invasion
– freezer hum, fridge shunting frustration
'round the corner, a distant plane
murmuring through a clouded skyway,
my hot-press boiler's morning gripes,
and in my ears persistent
hash brown static, scratching.

Yet, body haunts me; haunts
places I have been,
each where I want to be;
makes me solid and important –
this invisibility it is – undressed,
and lost in time's pinhead.

Go, haunt this universe I cry –
though I suspect you'll not stop by
again to be hello, nor take
my hand to bid adieu.

Day 5

Ghost

The centre of mass will out
so vaulting you will clear the bar.
If I carry a ghost with me it is you.
I might perhaps undress your shadow,
part it from you, from your body
and host it on my pathways,

in my rooms: – to be
a shadow-weave to spar with,
a skin cast to slip a smile on,
to whisper to a loving,
to shout at, or breathe with,
your ghost language ever rhyming.

That and this too: three times you:
my you, ghost you, and, you.
If not returning, this is my you;
otherwise, why this shadow-bait?
Here, take my thirsty snake belly
and my history – to expiate.

Day 6

the down and the then

out there –
 complete yet unfinished
out there –
tearing here to bone
if I could stand up
from this pen and to it
as it comes into itself
I would stand still
think through necessary thoughts
let clothes spot from my shoulders
drop to earthen floor
seek in my naked
a who with flesh to undo, to uncoil
to flay itself from bone lie by my feet
in bloodied wellings that soak into
the down and the then
see – skeleton me lost
in a standing of bones flowing to ground
odours of clay in the muscle of leaf
riddling on bark and bole leaking
branches to be among

Day 7

Outside

A yellow ambulance,
turns carefully into distant traffic,
framed in my half-open window

Pepper snapping raindrops
fly the wind.
Moaning rises from the river

by a flat bridge; there the road too
is flat, and this sky. Below,
sixteen wet timber garden

benches soak their solitude
as workers ghost past the evening
umbrella'd and scarfed in vain.

A pair of swans slip by upon
the darkly under-bridge water
to some world-without-end beyond.

Day 8

The clothes basket

Beside the travel bag
an old wicker basket
is bedraggled, overflowing and miserable
– greying sheets, t-shirts, worn grey socks
humble on the lid.
The bedroom door is closed
and a-bed pen in hand
waiting is miserable too.
But hey, this black trimmed
travel bag stays pert,
sure of itself by the door.

Day 9

If I skip a beat on the piano

Today was an odd sort of day
that other day was one too.
I've dealt with oddity before;
there have been such days before.
But a new torque sharpens this today
which was the day before yesterday.

If I skip a beat on the piano
or laptop, it's gone and where
it must have been squats
visible and audible as a filling
of the emptiness that resolves
some unexpressed equation.

Leftovers subtracted may distract
but always taint the smokescreen.
Why is why so absorbed
I stroke utterly deceived
the rhythms in your skin.

This poem was made tomorrow not today

For TC

It was an odd sort of day.
Morning came with a splish of sunshine
to glisten wet pebbles and tiles.
Starlings rhyme the roof and gable nest.
I stop-step downstairs, put the kettle on,
table plate and porridge bowl
to dine, my guest and me,
on words and wheat. He
all fired up on fuels of injustice
me dampened down, and slow.
Stuff on my mind, hours in my way.

By night-time returned, business done,
answering a friend on the phone
about the day's monotonies, I say,
'It's been an odd sort of day.'
The phrase becomes a T-junction
we wait by 'till he counters with:
'That's it! – an odd sort of day,'
adding, beyond the silence,
'Take it – let 'er run.'

Day 11

Words written

Cock o' the Walk. Talking the talk.
And dead beat.

Perhaps like a flat Guinness in a slow glass
there's little point in talking.

Imagine – or pretend
but note the crowning facets, the broken serifs.

Words on paper if heard at all,
spin like dice and halt

as surprised falls of vertigo
into unsatisfactory rhymes.

Day 12

Spinning

At a slant – yes. Polarised,
battered by weather outages,
tornado, cyclone, hurricane,
soft rain and now warm
sunshine?

Though I have sprouted
from the globe, on your map I list
to starboard and lose myself
for nothing else is upright
not a mothering bartering
globe glob tiny thing...

It was not you of course,
but Emily
– at a slant.

Day 13

Ways of Knowing*

*"He threw away his shield to be
A naked I."*

– SEAMUS HEANEY

Word-free, we came in order not to be elsewhere.

It was in the year of the gathering too
so even the crows perched on high
cawed their hymns to Sirius –
resting on the very edge of words.

It is not easy to escape
a presence
to the absence that there is
in coffins.

Thomas Aquinas stained his share of bone
and in a kind of ecstasy proclaimed
all he had done, "mere straw". He wrote no more.
Ways of knowing live above or underground.

"Take the fire of the beloved," Rumi said
"and leap with joy" – express the shining breath of day.

Word-free, we came in order not to be elsewhere.

* Written for the lost Quarterman Manuscript of poems in Tribute to
Seamus Heaney by Irish poets. Heaney quotation from 'An Open
Letter'.

Rock Written

Swanie's brain is flat and slatey.
The cluttered cloudy mesh he's seen
in not so brainy magazines or text books
is a clump of grey-white stuff,
we don't call flesh, graffiti'd,
bubble'd, scratched and written on.
Not easily reworked nor teased
into appeasing moulds.
Graptolitic: is that why? Rock-written.
Analysis and measurement
for modelling are difficult
and we are a hard people:
we think in saw-blade streaks,
carbonised, unrelenting; unforgiving
sacral incubi on the shore in shards.
But in tap-taps of the fluid geologist
hammer, fragility reveals what Swanie
now observes: – on time, the tide is never out.

Loft overflows

A once nourishing harvest of life,
its weather warm and moist,
brewn through rusty decades, unlaboured
like the scythe, tractor and thresher
in field and yard.
Uncle Henry's loft is empty now,
dusted everlastingly in bypassed
seed between dry-warped boards.

Once from atop these lofty stone steps
my brother Mike, curious at seven,
found a nest of newly hatched
and tested their capacity for flight.
He tossed from his palm, one by featherless one,
the full clutch, skywards from the high doorway.
Each helpless cheeping thing flat dived
to cobble stone below.

Though loosely fostered bodies now loiter
its walls, and an old sofa sits unemployed
in this vaulted long forgotten void,
that timbered floor once bulged to the rafters,
leaked through door and window, bubble-
heaved, breath-full, ripening and alive,
labouring atop those high-up stone steep steps
until somewhere en route, time bent its wattled neck.

Day 16

Prodigal

for Don Mullan's ISLAND OF IRELAND 'Christmas Truce & Flanders Peace Field' project

Prayer is mattress for their night
a curse its hidden wound

It has been a cold season on earth, in the sky;
in between where men hide or cry in the dark,
the night is listening. Vested in barbed wire,
silence curdles. Rumour fuels the burning time
though all seems quiet now...

until, across the way, the whisper of a light.
Then sleeping men awake and huddle to the top;
some soften with a thought, strain to thaw their shadows.

Like a garden pathway blossom, a distant light takes root
and multiplies as hedgerow whitethorn sculls
a laneway for some long lost prodigal
journeying home, alone.

Prayer is mattress for their night
a curse its hidden wound

Then each man rises – bird in flight – man alone,
wings curving with currents on the move
and each man soars in the strange inviting sight
of this sharp night, each man alone a man in flight,
hosting dread and fear in skyward thrusts of faith
and hope before the noise to come.

Then, a soldier drops his gun. And another.
Others, understanding, wipe an eye. Then on and on those dead
men file to sing on no-man's-land as madness
stills the world awhile, unchurns the mud, unbinds
the shackles of the dark.

Prayer is mattress for their night
a curse its hidden wound

Day 17

Catastrophe turnings

Waiting in a not knowing
as ground shakes, shifts and crunches
where below sea roars lift
curving winds across our cliff.

Migraine imbalance, or vertigo,
this tiny village floor, wobbly
on its vast ascending plug of rock,
rotating, floating free it seems
but briefly for it agitates
a thunderdown to silence.

It will rise again.
Turn-table round and back,
round and back, until incontinent
its thunderous hum down plunges
hard to ground.

– Catastrophe, this abc hatching
sinister as waves untackle cliff scales.
Movement palpitates again, hovers
in this swaying head, upward, backward,
around, until slung through
some sudden shaft of thought
that then subverts the mind
to spin a panic rim, desperate as a ninth
wave surge of knowledge crests,
all logic gone. Malevolent.

Fragments of apocalypse
set Yeats's beast and Christ's
cross on new horizons
in fraught postmodern
battlefields of today,
dead gods and mud everywhere;
you – and me – nowhere.

Chaos – riverine, elastic, warped,
and casual, has furrowed
unfamiliar canyons
in re-veined ground.
Darkness unanswered
asks what waking currents
must there be still to come?

Day 18

Estuary

A short pacy walk seemed right
for this mild post-windblown night
and I late rising, late arriving.
Across the estuary road below the park
looking left, then right – no traffic.
No-one at the waterline before me.
To my right in pairs, duck-like gulls
croak in unison at one older beak.
Soulless greys of sky and water hide
a watching heron that shies below,
spreads unhurriedly its floppy wings:
duotone browns brush the low horizon
as it slants into an easy glide
of fifty yards or more.
                              Upshore a mate
entwines their flights in curving arcs
that simultaneously dip then part
to settle on separate onshore rocks,
landing spots that I must now eschew.

Day 19

The old cartwheel

Sitting here in the afternoon's latticed window envious of the light, sensing folds of wind spirited as ash-leaf undersides beguiling time, the new cartwheel Jim Mahony made – in his village workshop by the churchyard, smelling of timber shavings, wood peels comforting the floor we flee as children will the sizzling steam from its peg-hammered iron rim-band and remembering the shaped smoothness of its spokes ready for roads, lanes, dirt boreens and the hard rough fields – betrays no surrender now lying here among wrinkled nettles and cowslips, balanced on its heavy hub, freewheeling in my mind.

Nothing much happens

Today I love you.
The dog barking in my garden
belongs to a neighbour
– *dog shit again, Anne Hartigan!*

Time flips itself, already 'tis tomorrow
So I out my watch and back clock
one hour. I could fall in love
in that space – or out of it.

Justine, Balthazer, Montolive, Clea.
'...for some men nothing is written
unless they write it,' Al Aurens of Arabia.

Dying, like drying, is about time. Tonight
the radio said someone aged seventy-one
had died. It happens. I waited. For seventy-one.
But nothing much happens by waiting;
just the incidental: instances – accidents.
The ritual is what we await ... forms
of closure: coffin sizes, colours, death notices,
service sheets nicely typeset. And fresh underwear.
'Tis all processions, digging holes, casting clay,
beating down the sod with the backs of shovels,
'Just in case,' my mother used to say.

But if the notebook's not available
and the farmyard full, then
burn, baby – straight to the elemental
where on a cheap looking wall
of marbled alcoves, ugliness is truth.
And names are qualified.
Death is the inconveniences,

not a timetabling.
Time to go. Time to end. Time to not be.
Easily done, impossible to do.
Today I love you. Tomorrow
no promises. It may be windblown
and gusty in the morning.

Day 21

Owl

if the task is
Draw an Owl
and you know
there is no mouse
on the horizontal

let your busy hands
swish two ovals
one large, intersected
at its top
by the smaller oval

and at a slant to some
vertical you allow...

     – No.   No, no!

                      YOU
are the perch, the process,
and the OWL.

Composition

'Love, is man unfinished' Paul Eluard, trans. Beckett

Attention
focused
on layers of sound
flushes of colour or
smell-spurting slashes
will reveal its surreal
one breath at a time
in the marrow

In pressing and compressing
thought and word tender
motion becomes re-fleshed
in the bone's craggy alternatives
that is supposing there are bones
like in beef and mutton
If unintentional button up
self-lyric the rising flesh
in your reflection

Skin
notes binds expands contracts
leaks bleeds weaves and makes
sacral connection

Attachment
though perhaps constricted
is & is not
constructed

Attention,
like time, hanging
within itself as scaffold
until self-flayed
will field, fold and file
ruling things out
reeling things in

The Orb

These hands betray a feint tremble
as they shelter a release of breath
– this living weeping thing they hold
perplexed as you breathe deeply in.

Around it tease a weave of string,
a shoelace loosened in the chase,
to seal its worn and battered eyes
into secure goodbye.

A way to build, to walk again.
To heal, encase, to hold and know
so far as hands embrace
so this may be their tale.

Let gently go: for 'tis not war.
And weave its beauty moult to orb
invisible between those palms.
Breathe in until the healing heart expands.

Precursors

See, Roscommon's Maeve reciting,
as Ailill's out-stretched hand
pillows Kevin's blackbird
– story fissures in the telling.

That large white bath-towel
slung across the open door
dominates this en-suite mini-chamber
now encumbered by outside owl-

like whistle-screeching cries
that warn the fragile air.
Blue and white striped shirts hang
from doorknobs; shoes, stockings,

jeans and books stalk the shelves
in lives of questionable authenticity.
Fresh thought-splinters mine the floor
feet trust to reach a door.

Harboured in this much loved duvet bay,
no longer in bellies of pervasive whales,
upwelling counter-currents moil the splay.

Submitting as a palm-tree does

'Such things as children see and store up to fortify or disorient their lives.'
    – Lawrence Durrell

A camel collapsed from exhaustion outside the door.
Too heavy to bring to the slaughter-house.
Men with axes appear in the open street
to cut it up then and there. They slice through
the white flesh, the camel thrown on its side,
living and dying. Pained, aristocratic
and puzzled as leg after reddened leg
bleeding freely is hacked through, struck off.
Then the rising neck and head, eyes open – pupils
that look from their dark. No protest, no voice,
submitting as a palm-tree does to its fall.
The street clay soaks the spreading blood,
and prints from bare feet tile the ground
with tales alive in the odours of night
but lost in the street choked gutters next day.

To the naked woman in the far window

'... ... the foot is more noble than the shoe, the skin more beautiful than the garment with which it is clothed,' Michelangelo said. But who will claim the why we gaze: the beauty sought or the pursuit? So, I might place you on a cold altar slab in Ambrosia, *pace* Praxiteles. Your shoulders, buttocks and heels to the stone, undressed too, to tempt a sacrificial toll, nakedness elevated unto nudity, flesh become word, each syllable a haemoglobin of desire or promise – but

if by chance

you are

looking

unless

you have hawk eyes, or binoculars,

you could

not know,

as the

sun sculpts

and warms my

face, that

though I lean

to almost kiss the kitchen

window glass, my worshipful

eyes are   eyes are

closed   closed

made of clay naked or clay dressed ambiguities attend your presence, your promise is to undermine the squalors of belief. Entangled in the physics of stone. Here are words the body made, Fish. Fowl. Flesh. Unwashed, unguents stickily sweet but smelling too of roses. Here is the aroma of ritual; no miracle to come. In the pew sits a wounded lion, mane magnificent and speared tail tapping the clean mahogany bench.

Still life on water

October 24

These sycamore falls are canvas worlds
in brown and yellow, dappled,
matte, rich pastel bright. No wind
now – and tidy; clean swept
brush-stroke waves strap the gutters,
hairbrushed to the shoulders and nape
of a long curved and leaf lined day
on the North Circular Road.

But (Buck) Jones's Road is leafless;
the wind blew all the way past
stadium and hotel, sweeping clean.
Under the slow bridge gliding swans
tease me to an unexpected curiosity:
two swans aswim at a slant to the bank.

The lead swan imperceptibly adjusts
direction towards a mesh of fallen leaves,
a densely bonded island float
held on the canal's dark undercurrent.

The darkness now seems destination or hiatus,
as the lead swan tacks into the leaf-lake
rippling its meniscus to a rise and fall,

spreading out those leaves
which backflow to bond again
leaf on leaf, broaching
a still life on water.

I move on – across one bridge,
and underneath another, wondering
if swans die on their own.

Day28

Fractality

Frack is = to the power
of water under air.
I is = to silence (in parentheses)

Toxic exhalation from subcutaneous infection
+ time is ≤ consequences detected.
Undeclared implies unknown
but is = to unspoken. [Buried. Toxic.]

I imagine fragmentation

Fragments sound bright; often are:
things that spin gallantly, galactically,
leaking boundaries, displacing grace
like unloved words that will persist
and occupy space, seldom harmlessly.
Or cauliflowers.

But fracked feels deep
and painfully chamfered.
Fractures inevitably expand
and/or contract.
We work our steel, evacuate

the belly of the earth,
re-colonising in parentheses
its rocks, its oils, its airs.
No longer turning clay
to harrow,
seed or grow.

When I see those faces

When I see those faces
and note the inward note-taking
I am satisfied.
We are somehow in tune.
Out of body words adventure
on pages as copybooks close
and find time in their dark.

Poems behave like that – brute breath
burrows, embeds in paper to foment
as among flowers:
petals ennoble warrior hearts,
and perfume love's caress,

Day 30

The green lane

The green lane legs its new grass
　　strides from here to all along
where unfenced fields are healing
　　wounded ground's up-risen bellies
swollen in the yellow of the come
　　and go we bring across
the ache of hidden ways, in canyons
　　of silent air in bird song
to where we know not to lie but yet
　　to lay aloud and there to be
on common straw where the lips
　　of night will suck away the sun,
and leave us shelling words
　　to flesh the stay of home.

Day 31

I

Be still

Turn this page

II

Slowly
mind that circled centre

Truth, though momentarily unbearable
will give release, enable integrity,
lighten your burden.

Wait a silent finger-count to ten
and then
look up
to where it's waiting
to be let in.

Now, turn the leaf

III

IV

Breathe in
        Breathe out
– and gently
              let it go.

Now, pass on
  or
  if you will:
        RETURN

Day 32

Ambiguities

I've known for ever, yet only know just now:
The sun that brought this morning slipped away.
The moon it drew beside, faint in colder sky, must soon follow.
Ambiguities. And returns that will not be... What's to decide?

This window frames its beehive combs; the ice cold startles painted trees
into some smiling autumnalty of brittle yellows.
So bright.   How was the night?
The yet to come is somehow bolder, and consuming everything
     of me there is –
Already leaving me behind
who never shirked to run, climb or page
words that passion-kiss this fibrous clay.

History seasons architectures, spices sage and parsley.
Sit there – love – sit there, 'twill not be long. Heart's truth,
     this shoulder is strong.

Lullaby for Words

Hear these words in your sleep
Hear these words as you dream
Hear these words fill the air that you breathe

Say these words as you sleep
Say these words in your dream
Say these words about water and fire

Be these words in your world
Be these words with your skin
Be these words as you grow into you

These words are
      Love in your heart
      Truth in your mind
      Sunshine to brighten your day

(Echo x3)
Love in your heart
Truth in your mind
Sunshine to brighten your day

Day 34

Listen to the blue

And bring this body
covered in its shroud of meaning
to a place of stone and clay.

Wake it underneath an open sky
lulled by watching cloud
or washed in winter rain.

There is the expectation of decay
into molecules of time
– thought we float upon or filter through;

and the evaporation of desire.

When desire is gone
what further need to know,
what means to be

in any form we know … nor any love?

Memory belongs to you who know
that one who was, was here
breath free – clay nourished

a rabbit snared or wolfhound
leaping mountains. Semi-quavers lost
to hands that touch, skin that tells,

to nose that smells, ears that sigh,
to eyes and mouth in thrall
to some magnificence.

All other songs, songs unsung
in blood now gone,
mere markers of a flow.

Empty or full
Here was.
Now is nought.

Let silence unveil a splendid night;
draw breath, sound a note
and listen, to the blue.

Day 35

Flowers of the baobab tree bloom at night

Knarled its bark
knarled its bite
knarled its motion
sometime cave
for the poacher.

Where one stands
horizons are long
sunshine strong – so strong

Knotted, hardened
– a breathing tower
its forest a dark
speckled welling

Terrible stillness
terrible centredness
terrible awning
fruit in shelter
up high – up high

near to the sky
so near – so here
on the ground

O – where the sun
where the night
what this dawning
muscle of life

holding twilight
rising pride
a savanna lion
with a great black mane

Baobab
          See.
A baobab tree.

V
Talking down the clock

'When I perhaps compounded am with clay.'
Sonnet 64. William Shakespeare

Prologue

This end of time is merely
end of me. So I have learned
and do in part believe it.

I

– blast and worse!
it cannot be THAT time. Language
doesn't help. Time insists
on its own ratcheting.

Silent regulator of heat, cold,
noise, skin, machining.
Patron of the now and then.
Damned mechanised soul-drop.

Time maps for its own intent
(though legitimate in this instance,
being a wall-hung central heating timer,
sentinel and guardian to my kitchen).

Not mine, those rhythms. Mine are
irregular, uncertain, and my own business;
yours linear, uncurved and smotheringly
unwound – so

Stop!
   Clock. Stop!
       Stop!

When
light and water
hide from darkness,
and all ablaze a setting sun
is threshold to the night, sky emerges
lintel to its rising dawn. In sleep the world
turns upside down and day's embrace unwinds.
One might then hear a pen scratching, see
the paleness of the ink, feel the earth's
crust sanding down its fingernails,
and wonder why we wake
so unremarkably:
the
where
we've been
woven on the breast
of night, making strange
the moment of its indeterminate
now, unmarked; a locket pendant in
oblivion's pearly-misted skin.

Oyster Catchers beak
seaweed – the wind and ripples
scissor-search wet sand.
Time corrugates its own ripples
zesting evening shadow
as you walk wavelets
that lap Portmarnock beach

Stop!
   Clock. Stop!
       Stop!

There is no one at the door
no one in the hall,
no one on the stairs.
The bathroom – empty;
the bedroom too.
This kitchen serviceable but cold
and in a room to thrive in,
all is silent
even with the radio on.
No one coming to the gate.

There is hesitancy in the air
as if the curtains shore the draughts
lest movement tell the why.
One is tempted to a laugh.
Where is there to dismount?
No where to sit down.
Empty couches chair rugs,
a lone log makes fire.

Stand, walk – walk, stand. Maybe
random skip a line to reach
the window, stopping to look
through the wicker-weave of night.
A still moon silent, in no hurry
through amber leaves of light.

As if in epilogue a recognition:
those leverets did not
return this spring to the park
below my window,
and I
– looking out for morning,
mid-day or evening rhythms –
absorb that colophon.
Those unsung notes.
Maybe they hibernate
or migrate those leverets
their rhythm loping new rhymes.

Orchids in the kitchen
wither, fainting slowly
in hidden falls of wilted whiteheads.
In the bedroom a black duvet cover
bides fresh nights on wine-red sheets.

Stop!
    Clock. Stop!
            Stop!

In this shell's disintegration
we pierce flesh with thorn
we relish and absorb storm
and though poisons brew
beneath the revelations of each day
last night's emptied rubbish bins
– refuse & recyclables –
had been wheeled into space
between houses and neatly parked
– by some neighbour

it was raining
the house was warm, the dark gentle
to feet on cold stone
ambition disappeared
and for a while sting stalled
happy to bide until the eye
found serpents asleep
on the stairs return.

I cannot read those eyes
there is no expression in this face
silent touches hold
tell of some want
in a gaze wholly political
not social – one that must not
be asked what might there be
for me.

It is hard to hold together
past, present and future
without saddle and reins.
Spurs and whip sharpen thighs
Like a spark of nitric oxide
but pencils lose their points
indifferent to will be or was
if time is blinkers and bit.

This right palm and right foot hinge
a mythic stave. Not crucified, yet
fixed to bar, your body's swing and sway
in perfect pitch; a silent stay
you are the between space, the door
awaiting motion wave through you
to shake and rattle bone in blushing skin.
This ghost town desert a masthead
serving no entrance, offering no exit.
Is it that the universe needs you to stop
its draughts from time to time, to tune
as it draws breath for cosmic song
phrasings of love and hate, minor keys
that let you be, flapping naked, hanging on?

Stop!
   Clock. Stop!
          Stop!

There was no revolution
no one sang; and train tracks seemed
an ok place to sit by and wait;
– no guitar in sight; warm air
brimmed to overflow a melodic
cowling for our ears;
silence bursting now to converse
to breathe an urgency,
a commotion.

But no one moved,
even as a train passed by
pulling itself through.
That seemed to suck all
in its after-draught,
and the silence emptied.

On a crest nearby we watch
a solitary figure fall to ground
crumpling slowly inward

in dreamlike fugitive collapse.
That disturbance leaves each
alone, and without
expectation.

Stop!
   Clock. Stop!
      Stop!

II

There is always a divine rite
for things we peddle:
'the rinds of the midden-heap'
the here there near or far
as we trudge wooden bridges
blindfolded, enscarfed and tangled
in a pride of goats unfazed
by an executioner's sword.
O silent heart –
Stay, stay.
                What else can be amiss?
The colours in this shirt? The size
of shoes? The last of beaten gold?
Stop to look this way... and if you come
listen ... you who follow close

Necklace'd in cold cascades the chill
of solitude's joy is here, aware,
plunger of steel, tonguing deep
a decomposing kiss.

All this wrinkle flesh wet, dry,
and hair, and nails rough and ready
to tease my back. Scratch harder.
To know, we hold.
Face composed,

sunlight between thighs
eyes of jade, worm-silk cheek bones,
belly-rise; nipples sideways, afloat
as fingers feel and file each fold
to store for winter.

And if you must, to face truths
hovering on your shoulders,
would you dismount,
would you abandon time?
For who, coursing a new arc
will score, through-composed,
uncharted swamps, or will refrain
where tigers bay fearless coughs
and swans elegantly couple.

Stop!
   Clock. Stop!
      Stop!

When the sanctuary lamp
enkindles anger it is time
to muse on everyday rituals,
to dance between the pillars of the house,
to make love by the airport road.
In the morning you may recall
this moon stands a Venus risen.

Over the way sits a hare
marking boundaries we cannot breach
stare as we will. Sunlight springs
its spirited arc in long for'ms
across the angular grass.
The vault is hollow
and darkness squanders
the stillness of high ears.

When marking boundaries
on our reach of time

is it too late for kindness?
What's left but sit
adrift among drowsy words
not a solitary cross in sight;
last night's moon still there,
the morning spilling
its hard cold air.

As you cross pathways to enter
the woods, soft verge grasses
imprint your passage
concrete slabs that flank
the route remain anonymous
and you?   You disappear.
There is hope in teasing inner walls.
Impossibility softens
under a steady gaze.
Scale with confidence
this close inevitable universe
for in a moment's narrative
it parts.

There is no bus-stop on this run,
no ready stopping what's begun.
No punching holes through hidden walls
to find where I have left myself
and verify a passing through.
No corroboration that I am
en route.

Stop!
    Clock. Stop!
        Stop!

He's patrolling the borders of my way
el lobo baying for my thought
but he's uncertain of the ways I think
for him sink lines are parallel
sometimes square.

In our in-between spaces
arc opportunistic curves,
and dark wakes where one might hide
are forever fanning time with light
or designing tattoos for your breasts.

i do not need to simmer down below
it's a mistake to so presume;
el lobo will not wait the scent of flow
is analytic, catatonic, then gone
whereas i may or may not wait
may or may not sing a song

It is in the eyes. Yes. The eyes.
Aye or nay you are coming
– that I do believe
though fallen leaves may silence
all your colours.
For the road at an easy canter
sprint in yellows and blues of light.
There always is a where to go.
Yes. There is. There is.
– there is a where to go

Snow falling
on trees and grass
each flake frosting invisible
meniscuses dissolves sound
In winter snow is good
you are good – ah, colder than snow
yet more beautiful

On Knockmeldown's flank
early morning – evening late
sunlight flaunts the Vee
sunlight taunts the Vee
at Knockmeldown's mountain pass
shadows distract me

Evening shadows slope through silence
as sleep forgets the day's lines;
when memory slips through dawn light
cormorant and shag rise to the waves
flutter wings – are gone

Now I am river, borgesian tiger
coiling flame – river tiger fire
self-consuming burning bright
time-struck nature bed together
feeding our decay, variegated
as our weathering.

Stop!
   Clock. Stop!
          Stop!

III

Without knowing – long alone
and listen to the touch
of other bells' vibration.
Morning sunshine
between parted curtains,
light running through hillside
pathways hidden from the eye,
the call of dark at night,
the kiss without caress –
O sole mio, seal im aonar,
this tone-soft loneness
has no knowing.

Longing cleaves abandonment
to where nothing happens
– but, for a how long?
'Till light returns and swells
the where a lover spells
those palms of day.

Last week Steve;
earlier this year, Tom;
last year, Michael...gone.
Jarlath, Jan, Elizabeth, Gerry
imprinted Liffey signatures
unstitched, decommissioned.
Singing Diarmuid too has gone.
and yesterday the strong Michael O'Brien, a tree
fell in our forest of books. Silent.
We have strong feet, eyes, voices
but winter tunes relentlessly
the strings of time's elasticity.

Stop!
   Clock. Stop!
      Stop!

As winds flow our nakedness
and raindrops glisten skin
hair flattens and heads bow;
drop by drop we touch down;
like words spilled from books read,
imbibed and sentenced,
we forget desire.

There you go. Marching
as tomorrows swallow yesterdays
and open arms spell winter's ends
head proud as it was born,
strong heart step by step
Morning is no more

I notice the key on the table
while venturing a journal note
and drinking a slow breakfast of tea
from the dark green mug.

There are two distortions
in the angled moment, standing close

under light that slants through
the frosted panes of a door:
   hesitant hands – busy in code
rummaging handbag and pockets
in an exchange of glances
   questions – that pointlessly posit
matters of such consequence as
'Why is the curtain not drawn back?'
but never wait an answer.

Stop!
   Clock. Stop!
              Stop!

IV

'Poetry in South America ...
a different matter altogether.'
Neruda bloomed and he had rivers
without names, trees, and birds still
undescribed. The great man's 'Song'
had come open-eyed, worldly wise.

Below my room a harmless flotilla
of swift flowing Corrib bubbles
and swans feathered by the breeze
turn a corner into the wind.
Round the garden table
six will-be lovers wonder.
The cool wind hunching
their shouldered laughter.

This moment of movement.
Is this rebellion? This page.
How might it answer? This pen.
How might it spill or stain,
or suck marrowbone to know

what rocks to throw?
Revolutionary taunting haunts song.
The blows struck to strike out.
Intent drawing another clout.
What matter motives? Water flows.

All who squat here to trip the 'why'
sit up and spare the heart
get your ass off that chair
lay it bare – lay it bare
Perhaps the words to use are
not so common as the flags that fly
to spark an eye on destination
in some urbanised scurry
easier to blast to an infinity
than hamlets on mountainsides.
Revolution so so slow.
The cavities a heart will fill
to ease the mind's recession,
to lay it bare – lay it bare.
Trust in the seed of ritual.

Stop!
   Clock. Stop!
      Stop!

Tempus fugit. Time will stubborn on.
I neither believe nor comprehend
its ripostes, and must re-visit
to bridge voyages – for time leaks
through skin. The next is very slow
to come – the always not the now.
Anxieties of influence, precursors
real or imagined. O for a blunt
unsubtle antagonism.
Fear of verse contamination,
lines hitching up their mountainsides;
yet, there are radiations one might
wish darkened of a summer's night,

if only to be outraged by the fecundity
of dying, or the absence of distinction,
the why principles defy sincerity.
O the irony of it all. The loss. The superstition.
Knowing that in time, on time
it does no good to whine.
Yet, who does not love this crawl
through possibility, swimming
slowly, holding back the flood
in swirling parallel wakes.
This wave-lament, this oval lace.
But if you love, or have awhile,
or once, or almost so,
rejoice – let go lament and wake
celebrate what pushes time aside
each day, each hour; let time
confound itself into decay as you
arrive at this today 'when I perhaps
compounded am with clay'.

Stop!
   Clock. Stop!
      Stop!

Time local and time personal excite
each other into universal entanglement:
Today is still today when it is tomorrow
The cat is out of the bag. Ignorance is bliss.
The discovery of thought excites,
delights, reveals, words such as Nietzsche wrote
– the poignant beauty of life –
that on sharing will infuse memory
with love's timelessness, a cupful of infinity
that overflows, a spoonful of love's emotion
though storm winds rise and sky darkens.
Between the light and dark
our words betray, entwine, dismiss.
With bars removed and candle flame pinched out
we forward roll across time's hidden tipping point,
then lose sight, sound, taste, smell, and touch.

The joy of fetching one daisy from millions
whitening their hillside horizon'd lawn.
Time subsumes the mud we squander.
Of 'The Church at Zillebeke': 'in that mad
start of hell' – 'all that's left' was mud.
and yet we hold to joy as if time
is mollified by our transitions.

A droll elephant in dried mud
stands to spray its rump with sandy
micro-cosmic dust that disturbs
into darker matter, seducing space
and all its occupants onto
some other where.
A wolfishly difficult business
this time-keeping – time to read time
to raid time to tarry – by now clock
has forgotten the before and after words
but never abdicates.
It warps itself enwrapping now.

Am I creation? Or an act of repetition?
In search of some significance?
Is signature to this relentlessness
the only there that is for me?
Absorbed in medieval workings,
slave to rusted cogs and levers
lurching through its parties digital,
part fear, part laughter sliding
cross-legged and irreverent, collarless,
abandoning any where there is to go;
being by the by; asking why.

You see, it is not me – this we.
The time I have is me.
The ways we know we need to find;
new crossroads, footpaths, byways, or lanes
will find us out in time.

With narrative its grammar, current, and currency,
time is not alone. Space fills, spills
over, flows across the page and calls
on urchin tentacles to toll their fill
as they unfold routes to rhyme.
Across uncharted reaches,
at each rise ventured, indifferent
to our crampon'd soles,
time is itself
ab-
    seil-
ing
    time.
Perhaps my 'am' is other; and my time is me
within some boundary where there be song
in splashes, rivulets, and torrents
that massage skin, muscle and bone
into silencing
the diaphanous
of all our knowing.

Stop!
    Clock. Stop!
            Stop!

Notes

I: 'We all end in metaphor'. Metaphor is 'the achievement of intimacy' See Ted Cohen, Metaphor and the Cultivation of Intimacy, Critical Inquiry, Vol 5, No 1. (Uni Chicago Press, 1978)

II: 'Sórt aisling óg' A Version in English.
A kind of youthful vision
From the beginning / legs striding down my road / were shapely bold. / Fast moving too. / And the dress with them. / Very naughty too, / no question –. / My dear, my dear / What's left for me? / Only a lonely bed / and a lonely table; / and loneness within. / Saucy legs, young one. / And the best of life to you!

VII: 'He remembered telling her...' Found poem adapted from the novel, Welcome to Gomorrah by Niall Quinn (Wolfhound Press, 1995)

VIII 'The supermarket maw'. In P is for poetry (The O'Brien Press (2020)

IX 'Marcel Marceau knew better': Published in 30 Days hath September, 2016 (for 25th), an online suite, curator & editor, Patricia S Jones, Emeritus Fellow, Black Earth Institute.

XIII: 'Measurements'. Published in 'Poems for September' an online suite 2012, curated by Patricia S Jones, NY. *August 28th is the birth date of Liam O'Flaherty, novelist & short story writer (1896-1984)

XVII In E. Lynskey, editor, Census 3: The Third Seven Towers Anthology, 2012.

XXIII: 'for love is'. *Max Ernst (1891-1 April 1976). The poem draws on images & biographical notes in *Max Ernst a Retrospective*, ed. Werner Spies (Prestel & Tate London, 1991) and works encountered at the Tate. These include among others: no. 126, Forest and sun, 1927; no. 241, Bird 1947; no. 116, Two people and a bird, 1926 (Deux personnages et un oiseau); no 209, The Painter's Daughter, 1940. Samuel Becket on Max Ernst: 'I salute, briefly, with no empty words, the instigator of this great, constructive "No".' from a letter to Werner Spies, 1972 (p. 339)

XXV *Rupert Brooke (3 August 1887-23April 1915) at Byron's Pool with Virginia Woolf and friends. See Some Desperate Glory, Max Egremont, Picador, 2014, page 20.

For the young
'Embedded in my brain'. Written for Eoin Colfer's Laureate na nÓg legacy project: Once Upon a Place, edited by Eoin Colfer & illustrated by former Laureate na nÓg, P.J. Lynch (Little Island, 2015).

Keys from Palestine

Of these, 'Amer's Story' owes its narrative contexts to courageous reportage during the appalling military Operation Cast Lead by Israel into Gaza. 'Gilad' refers to an Israeli soldier captured by Hamas two years earlier along the Gaza 'border'. Amer al-Helo was interviewed in February 2009 by Eva Bartlett, a Canadian human rights advocate and freelance journalist who published his story, "They killed me three times" in Live from Palestine, 24 February 2009 (The Electronic Intifada). Poem first published in Lynskey, ed, Census 3: Seven Towers Anthology, 2012.

'What there is'. Commissioned for the Mamilla International Poetry Festival, and also read in Mamilla Graveyard, Jerusalem's ancient Arab burial grounds, alas almost entirely build upon by Israel with grievous disrespect for both living relatives and the interred. In Poems for Mamilla: The English language poems from the Mamilla International Poetry Festival, Ramallah, 2013; organised by the Mahmoud Darwish Museum & ARCH (Alliance to Restore Cultural Heritage in Jerusalem) (The Otherworld Press & ARCH, 2014; ISBN 978-0-9576854-1-3)

'A fruit stall by the Hebron road'. These oranges did not tumble down the hillside of their own accord however; a passing military truck had stopped, trashed the farmers' stalls, overturning tables of fruit and vegetables, and then drove on. 'Going to ground'. In Gene Barry editor curator, Blackwater Poetry online, 2014

'Lifta Voices': Irish Times, Poem of the week, 30 Nov 2019

'Caoineadh Amjed of Beit Omar': written for the anthology, Palestinian Dead through Occupation, Turangalaila Palestine edited by John Ennis & David Mallaghan (2019). In memory of Amjed Bahjet Alami, a Hebron graduate journalist photographer, murdered outside his office by soldiers in a revenge killing because some children had thrown stones at their tank here on the previous day (see The Resting Place of the Moon by Felicity. Heathcote, p. 108, The Otherworld Press, 2007).

Daily Breaks

Day 19: 'The old cartwheel'. Poet Tom Conaty proposed a new poetry form, triggered by an Ikea meter strip available to customers. Ideally, best appreciated as one long line, so typographical experimentation is essential. Rules: a poem in one sentence, of 100 words (to include poem title, text and poet's name), along a one meter strip.

Day 20: 'Nothing much happens'. An irresistible nod to 'Neighbourhood Watch' a poem about 'doggy shit' by Anne Le Marquand Hartigan in Something beginning with P, ed. S Cashman (O'Brien Press, 2004), and in selected edition, P is for poetry, 2020).

Day 33: 'Lullaby for words'. Written as the closing piece for a words & music performance with poet Tom Conaty and singer songwriter Kalichi Donahue at Annaghmakerrig, April 2018 where it had its first public outing.

Day 42: 'Flowers of the baobab tree bloom at night' Forests of baobab trees in Tanzania fill me with delight. This majestic lion of trees in Tarangeri National Park, but under climate change threat.

Part V: Poem: 'Talking down the clock': 'A current scientific best interpretation of time measurement', according to Adam Mann in LiveScience July 14, 2020: "The smallest conceivable length of time might be no larger than a millionth of a billionth of a billionth of a billionth of a second." (Adam Mann, LiveScience July 14, 2020)

Section III of poem: deceased colleagues and friends from the publishing world named in verse 3 of section III, include: Steve McDonough (Brandon Press founder); Tom Turley from Irish University Press; Michael Adams, also IUP; Jarlath Hayes, designer, illustrator and typesetter). Our Book of the Liffey creators: Elizabeth Healy, editor of Ireland of the welcomes in its best days; and author. Jan de Fouw, designer, artist & illustrator. Gerard O'Flaherty, editor, Joycean reader and scholar; expert on Dublin, its history, literature and places; a true Dubliner himself. Beloved Diarmuid Ó Cathasaigh, walking companion of many years, club and folk singer, booklover, gaelgóir, raconteur, close friend, enabler of unending conversations. And in 2022, Michael O'Brien, founder of The O'Brien Press, competitor and close colleague throughout my publishing career and afterwards. All have been significant contributors to Ireland's book publishing industry and culture.

Acknowledgments

My thanks and appreciation to several colleagues, friends, poets and family (and especially my daughter Soracha) who kindly read some of this collection's works at various stages of the book's composition and construction. Their thoughts and time were generously shared, supportive and valuable. My thanks to all at Salmon Poetry for publishing this volume, especially to Jessie, Siobhán and Dani. Salmon Poetry has enhanced and energised poetry publishing in Ireland. Long may it thrive! Long may it talk on through the clock.

Notes on the Front and Back Cover Images

Front Cover: Janus Horse Head Sculpture, on a plinth, Tallow, Co. Waterford (Photo S. Cashman, 2022).

Legend on plinth: Is minic a dhein bramicáin giobalach capaillín cuimhasach / A raggedy little colt will often become an elegant young horse (Irish proverb)

Created by sculptors at the International John Hogan Memorial Sculpture Workshop, Tallow, Co. Waterford August/September 1991. Unveiled on 17 September by the recently elected President of Ireland, Mary Robinson.

The workshop, opened by Dutch sculptor Jack Verbrugge, included participant sculptors from Ireland, England, Canada, Sweden and Japan. The chosen motif was the horse, appropriate as since 1910, Tallow hosts an annual horse-fair. My father began his teaching career in Tallow, and nearby is my home village, Conna, Co. Cork, also on the banks of the river Bride, a tributary of the Blackwater.

The janus-headed horse figure brings to mind a childhood pride watching my Uncle Batty riding a horse called Old Conna at the local Ballynoe races. The sculpture's modernist or perhaps post-modernist design, with its plinth sides sculpted and decorated in horse motifs, ribs of iron, carved horse tails, and other symbols radiates the energies of folk art. The horse heads are in conflict and debate, and on this book, embrace the warm antiquity of the massive baobab tree on the back cover.

Back cover: Baobab tree, Tanzania (Photo Seamus Cashman, 2017)
The Baobab is a broad-trunked gigantic tropical tree (Adansonia digitata) of the silk-cotton family, native to Africa. Its flowers bloom at night, and its fruit, edible and acidic, is used generally for food and also for medicinal purposes. The bark is used in making paper, cloth, and rope. This particular giant is probably several hundred years old; baobabs can live for 1,000 years

SEAMUS CASHMAN taught in Tanzania in the 1960s, and back in Dublin became an editor with Irish University Press. In 1974 he founded Wolfhound Press to publish works of fiction, anthologies of poetry, cultural & literary studies, photography, history, and also quality books for young readers. He also reissued many established Irish writers of the early 20th century, including in particular: Liam O'Flaherty, Margaret Barrington and Monk Gibbon. Cashman introduced the public to the famed Father Browne photographs, with works on Ireland, the Titanic, World War I and Australian images. His Wolfhound Press won many book and design awards and earned a reputation for its contribution to the flourishing of Ireland's small press publishing through the 1970s to 2001. He received the Reading Association of Ireland's Special Merit Award in 2005 as compiler and editor of the children's anthology, Something beginning with P.

In addition to his poetry writing, Cashman also facilitated creative workshops with adults, teenagers and children, including in primary and secondary schools. At Zion NS, Rathgar, he collaborated with the Principal and fellow poet, Tom Conaty, to produce a children's film (Stitched) based on workshops with the children who wrote the entire script, and who helped produce and perform it for the film. For 2020, 2021 and 2022, he compiled and edited the extraordinary Poetry Ireland annual 'Poemathon' of response lines from the public to opening first lines on current themes by President Michael D Higgins; John Sheehan of the Dubliners; and former president and member of The Elders, Mary Robinson.

Cashman has read his poetry in Ireland, England, Belgium, the USA, Palestine and Saudi Arabia. He was an English language judge for the International Mamilla Poetry Festival at Ramallah, and their first International Fellow at the Black Earth Institute, a writers and artists think-tank in Minnesota, where he also edited the Peaks & Valleys issue of their About Place Journal.

Born in Conna village in East Cork, in a room his mother named 'Beggar's Bush', he has lived in Portmarnock, Malahide, and now Swords, in north Dublin since the 1970s. He has four adult children and a grandson, Conor, 'whose presence affirms the poetry of life'. His published work is listed on page four of this book.

salmonpoetry

Cliffs of Moher, County Clare, Ireland

"Publishing the finest Irish and international literature."
Michael D. Higgins, President of Ireland